GREEN
MOUNTAINS *and*
ROCK RIBS

Books by Keith Warren Jennison

GREEN MOUNTAINS and ROCK RIBS

Stories and pictures arranged by

KEITH WARREN JENNISON

New York

HARCOURT, BRACE AND COMPANY

LIBRARY OF CONGRESS CATALOG CARD NUMBER: 54-11325

LITHOGRAPHED IN THE UNITED STATES OF AMERICA
BY THE MURRAY PRINTING COMPANY, WAKEFIELD, MASSACHUSETTS

FOR MY BROTHER NED

GREEN
MOUNTAINS *and*
ROCK RIBS

I

There isn't much to see in this town...

but what you hear makes up for it.

2

What a beautiful view that is!

Maybe, but if you had to plow that view, harrow it, cultivate it, hoe it, mow it, fence it, and pay taxes on it...

it would look pretty durned ornery.

3

Used to be anybody could farm.

All you needed was a strong back...

but nowadays you need a good education

to understand all the advice you get so you

can pick out what'll do you the least harm.

4

They asked her how long the doctor said her husband
was going to have to stay in bed and she answered,

"Only one day at a time."

5

My car stopped a couple of miles down the road,
think you can fix it?

Sure can, I do everything from shoeing horses...

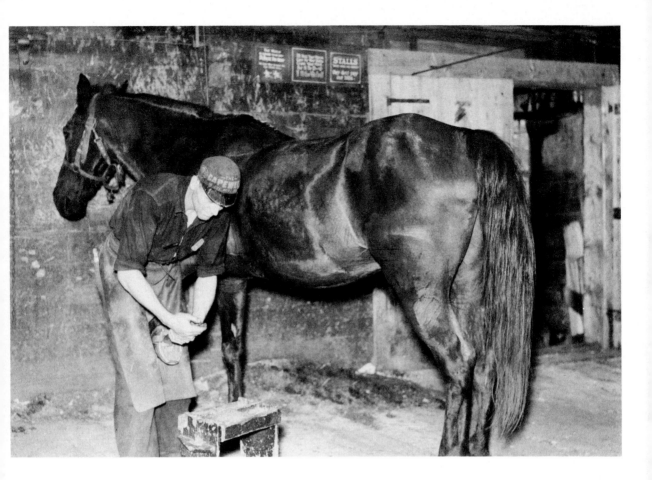

on down.

6

Most everybody around here knows what's going on...

but they read the newspaper to find out

who got caught at it.

7

Young Tommy Burton didn't speak a word until one day he was working with his father in the hayfield the summer he was ten years old. A bull from the neighboring pasture broke through the fence and when he lit out for his father,

Tommy yelled, "Look out Pa."

When they got back to the barn the father said, "Thought you couldn't talk."

"Never had nothing to say before."

8

The winters are long and the summers are short up here.

Just how short seems to vary from year to year. . . .

Last year it came on a Thursday.

9

How do I get on the road to Thompsonville?

Well, down this road about twelve miles there's a covered bridge . . . you turn off three miles before you get to it.

10

It took her twenty years to make a man out of her boy, and another woman twenty minutes to make a fool out of him.

II

Vermont may not look very big as states go, but if you got a flatiron and pressed it out it would be as big as Texas.

12

Joe Dawson, who came from northern Vermont, was visiting in Texas and he saw a strange bird run across the road in front of the car. He asked what it was and was told it was a bird of paradise. Joe thought for a minute and said,

"Kind of far from home ain't he?"

13

If a boy can pick two quarts of strawberries in an hour and a girl can do the same, any mathematician will tell you that a boy and a girl together will pick four quarts an hour.

While a farmer knows

they won't pick any strawberries at all.

14

I got a good-tempered man for a husband. Only mean thing he's said to me in thirty years is that he sure would hate to reap like I sew.

15

One of Henry Ashton's relatives asked him if his son who had become a movie star ever came back to the farm for a visit.

"Come back every summer for five years," said Henry; "brought his wife with him too...

five prettier girls you never saw."

16

You've got this farm in such good shape now, probably it'd run itself.

Sure would, downhill.

17

Thelma Jordan walked over to a car parked beside her orchard one day and looked in. The driver said, "Hello, can we take this road back to the city?"

"Don't know why not," said Thelma,

"you've taken 'most everything else."

18

A young stranger came up to the store one day and said it looked like it was going to rain.

One of the men said, "Nope, won't rain."

"Well those thunderheads are sure building up."

"Nope, won't rain."

"I didn't mean to start an argument, I just said it looks like it's going to rain."

One of the men asked, "What's your name?"

"Ed Perkins."

"Any relation to Jeff Perkins in Enosburg?"

"He's my grandfather."

"Any relation to George Perkins in Hardwick?"

"He's my uncle."

"How about Ned Perkins in Newport?"

"He's my father."

"Maybe it will rain."

19

One man from New York got to Woodstock after a big snowstorm. He couldn't figure out how to get across the street so he called over to a man on the other side. "How did you get across the street?"

"Born here."

20

Seth Mosely sure talked a lot at the town meeting last night—but he didn't say nothing.

21

Is it true there are more cows than people in Vermont?

Yup.

How'd that come about?

We prefer 'em.

INDEX AND PICTURE CREDITS